Do you sometimes feel scared of the dark?
It's perfectly normal!
But do you know that there are many reasons
why we shouldn't be afraid of the darkness
and we can even learn to like it?
Let's learn about some reasons to enjoy
the night time!

The stars shine brighter in the dark sky!
During the night you can see countless stars.

Look how amazing they are!

3

Do you like looking at the Moon?
The Moon, a true friend of our planet,
is so beautiful at night!

The crescent moon shines so mystical
in the dark sky.

You can play flashlight tag with friends
and tell amusing and exciting stories.

The calming bedside nightlight will help
you to soothe yourself to fall asleep.

You can observe and learn to identify constellations only in the dark. It is also an excellent opportunity to learn more about space.

You can make up your own space fantastic
stories looking at the millions of stars.

Tiny fireflies come out to play in the darkness. You can see them only at night.

The fireflies are like small living
flashlights that produce light
with their bodies.
Is not this amazing?
They are so cute!

It's a lot of fun to show different animals with a flashlight and your hands.

You can make up interesting stories and show your performances with shadow puppets in the evening.

Playing with a flashlight is always fun!

You can play flashlight tag with friends.
Reading with your flashlight is so cozy.

Marshmallows are especially delicious when you roast them over a campfire with your best friends.

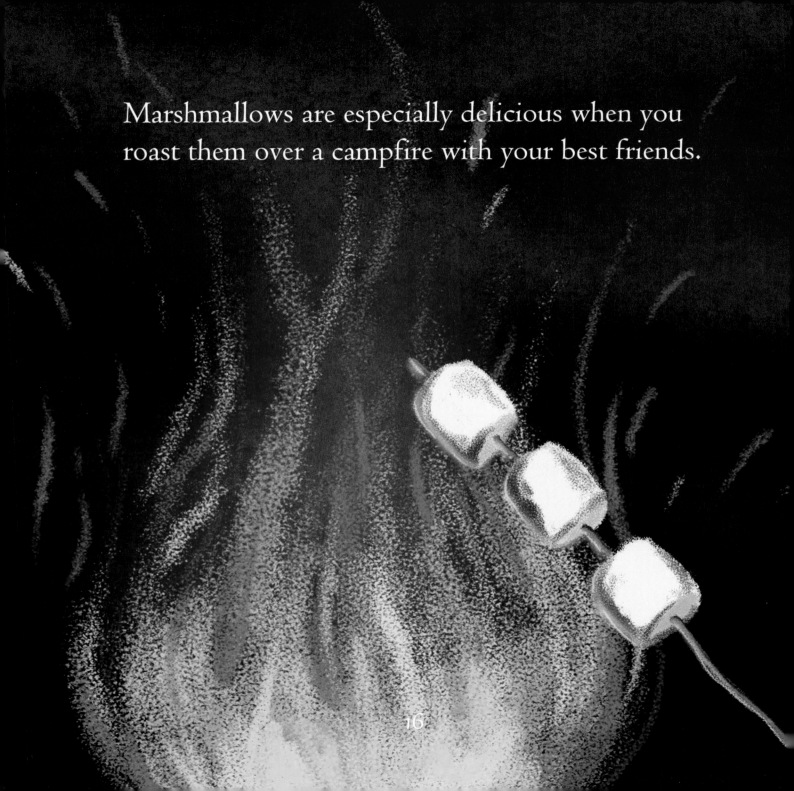

The darkness is the perfect setting for some spooky and funny stories around a campfire.

Do you like garlands?
There is always a magical atmosphere
in the room when you have garland
on you wall or over the bed.

Paper sky latterns glow so nice in the dark sky!

Cozy funny pajamas are another
reason to love the dark evening.
Do you have those pajamas?

You can also take your favorite toy
to the bed with you.

Our body and mind
relax in the dark.
It's time for thinking
about different things
you like before sleeping.

22

At night you can see your magical dreams.

So you see, the darkness is not scary at all!
You can do so many interesting and cool things
in the dark. Come up with another reason why
you can no longer be afraid of the darkness!

Made in the USA
Middletown, DE
01 March 2024